Sailing with the Wind

Sailing with the Wind

new poems 2023

Don Gutteridge

First Edition

Wet Ink Books
www.WetInkBooks.com
WetInkBooks@gmail.com

Sailing with the Wind
by Don Gutteridge

Cover Design – Richard M. Grove
Layout and Design – Richard M. Grove
Cover Image – by Sebosian, courtesy of Shutterstock,
        used by permission.

Essay by Miguel Ángel Olivé Iglesias, MSc

Typeset in Garamond
Printed and bound in Canada
Distributed in USA by Ingram,
        in Canada by Wet Ink Books

Library and Archives Canada Cataloguing in Publication

Title: Sailing with the wind! : new poems, 2023 / Don Gutteridge.
Names: Gutteridge, Don, 1937- author.
Identifiers: Canadiana 20230485480 | ISBN 9781989786949 (softcover)
Classification: LCC PS8513.U85 S23 2023 | DDC C811/.54—dc23

Table of Contents

Seven for Anne

Apple-Cheeked

For Tom, at one year, in loving memory

O my apple-cheeked boy!
I see thee still in the
leavening light of a May
morning, the bars of your crib
a-jib in your pistoning fists,
proclaiming to me and the world
that you are alive and thriving,
your infant curls like Apollo's
frothing locks, your eyes
as blue as agates in a jeweller's
glance, a-dance in their own
dappled delight, and the grin
you give me shivers in my soul
like a lover's embracing ache,
and will sleep there till the day
I too un-awake.

Pulse

For Grace Leckie

The girls of my country school
were slim-limbed lasses,
their locks braided, pixied,
coyly curled, and they joined
we boys, like lovable chums,
in the rough buffeting of rugby,
the daft dodgems of Prisoner's
Base or the skullduggery
of Behind-the-Back tag,
but Grace, one row over
was an un-chum with too
many swerving curves
to tumble tipsy, sprint
like a rabbiting rabbit or otherwise
weather our hodge-podge,
gender-free joustings,
and the glance she gave me,
across the grating acre
between us, had nothing of the
"buddy" in it, or the least
regard for my plumb-bobbing
pulse.

Patter

For my grandfather in loving memory

With Bob on one knee
and me bouncing on the other,
Grandpa begins: reciting
the oft-told tale of
of Goldilocks and the three
duped bruins – with a grrr
for Papa's outsized growl
and a pinched whimper for Mama
and a squeezed wee one for Baby's
trio of pleas, and who cared
that we knew every warp
and weave of the plot, for a story
was a story – our way of winching
the world a-right, and after
all is said and done,
it was Grandpa's patter that mattered.

On the Prowl

I loved to kneel beside
my bed, palms pressed
in penitent pose, and recite
the child's first prayer:
"Now I lay me down to sleep,"
but I was ever puzzled
by that penultimate line
about dying in the night
because I couldn't imagine
being unalive in the dark
with God on the prowl for souls.

Farewell

S.S No. 12: June 29, 1949
For Miss Nelson in fond memory

In this annual farewell
photo, wide-angled
to take in the tangle of faces
and forms of Miss Nelson's
final country-school
class: twenty-nine
of us scattered in eight
grades, in divers shapes
and thriving sizes, some
wincing at the sun's sudden
insinuation, others too shy
to blink or un-smile, and one
wee tad on the brink
of a giggle, while others, still,
pose for a parent or posterity,
getting into the swingof the occasion
(but my friend Coop
stands a-droop in the first
row, scrutinizing his boots)
and even after seventy years
have come and gone I don't
know where, I can name
a baker's dozen or two,
and whisper a belated prayer
for the woman who took us
on a furthering journey,
and taught us to love what we learned.

Cadenza

It must have been June because
the bugs of that nomination
were squeezing their scarobed, slug-
slung bodies upward
out of the home-loam
and into the rarity of Summer's
early air, wobbling
into lopsided flight
like big-bellied bombers –
seduced by the slick elixir
of light behind our bowed
window, and batting the glass
like frenzied Furies, and I wondered
what kind of demon-dance
dithyramed within, and played them
like a moon-mad cadenza.

Double Dutch

Point Edward 1948
For Butch McCord in fond memory

My best bud, Butch,
sometimes borrowed his father's
bike, and offer to take me
for a spin, and my Gran would say,
"Now, don't you go riding
double or you'll be in Dutch
with *Pedan," but I'd hop on the
hip-high crossbar
anyway, while Butch peddled
under it in lop-sided
commotion, and off we'd go
gee-whizzing from street
to street and alley to alley,
flouting the law with such
brimming brio, we felt
something akin to Eden's
flawed innocence, sallying
within.

*Constable Pedan was the
Point's lone lawman

Whimsy

There was nothing hallowed about
All Hallows Eve
in the Point, where infant witches
zoomed on borrowed brooms,
bleached-sheeted ghosts
hovered and haunted, clowns
with disjointed grins grimaced
till they giggled, skeletons, fresh
from the closet, rattled their home-
made bones, and Frankenstein
masks glowed like a moon-
gaffed gallows – embarking
all on the star-licked
dark in quest of candied
apples and caramelized kisses,
and the bliss of being something
other, and whimsically wicked.

A Bauble to Beguile

Point Edward: 1947

Withers' clapboard abode
stood on a double lot
with a lawn that rolled till it
greeted the street, where we played
croquet till the afternoon
weakened and the sun succumbed –
the envying air echoing
with the crack of our mallets on the
oaken orbs (sending them
hither or further than yon),
or the thwack of a winning roquet
and the victor's triumphal cry
as the striped stake is struck,
and we were young enough
to believe that games like these
were a gift from the only-begotten
gods, the inborn bliss
of the innocent, a bauble to beguile,
a bubble without a burst.

Perpetual

For a time, my only friend
was the goldfish, swimming
flimsy-finned in the glass
globe of his bowl, round-
about in clockwise
un-confusion, as if
he thought there was somewhere
else to go or a place
he ought to be or somewhere
fresh to set him free,
but when he got to the spot
where it all began, he met
himself coming back,
and I wondered what it might
be like to travel inside
a world perpetually circled,
without an end in sight
to make the miles worthwhile.

Inkling

For the girl-next-door

I mut have been a precocious
eleven, because the sight
of Shirley's curls, napping
on her nape, or the lithe lingering
of her girlish gams, sent
something beyond delight
brimming within, that could only
have been an inkling of my pre-
pubescent lust – the furtive
urge to bag and breed,
or, when Heaven's head
was turned awry, plotted
something naughty.

First Bike

Sarnia Township: 1948

I decided to take my brand-
new C.C.M.
for a spin on our country-bumpkin
roads, hitting every
pouting pothole I could see,
like Lucky Lott and his Hell-
driving paladins, scattering
gravel and flustering dust
in my wake, and I pedalled as pumped
as a Dominion-Day pacer*
until some perverse pebble
suborned my swerve, dumped me
in the ditch, and wiped the grin
from my face.

*Point Edward hosted
harness racing at the local track
every Dominion Day (July 1)*

To the Hilt

When January thawed, Leckie's
saturated fallow froze
right over, a glittering,
glazed membrane, swathed
in the moon's lavender flume,
broken only by the black
bulge of a far horizon,
where we skated like synchronized
sylphs. leaving, behind us,
filigreed fronds and the scarred
targets of our blades' bite,
and somewhere ahead,
where phantom winds wilted,
the world might vanish, but we
were addicted to speed and buoyancy
of bone, and welcomed whatever
the yawning beyond might bring
to those who hallowed to the hilt.

Bivouac

For Tom in loving memory

You came to us like a blue-
eyed gift from some
doting deity, and I wanted
so much for you to be one
whom the misbegotten gods
curried and coddled from womb
to grave, but it was not
to be: you lived your brief
bivouac on this blighted
orb with a kind of flurried,
geysering gumption, as if
the bloom that brightened it
was brave enough to un-
become, and gave you leave
to die.

Afternoons

The Withers abode stood
stoutly on a half-acre
lot in the thithering heart
of the village, and its capacious
lawns rolled fondly
down to greet the street,
and on warm summer afternoons
when the Lake was too cold
for toes or the naughty nuggets
of our nether region, we played
endless games of croquet,
with all the panache of grandees
grazing Versailles, or the madcap
dithering of Alice and her head-
lopping, crimson Queen –
knocking our misbehaving
balls a-thither when they ought
to be yon-ed, or tapping
belligerents beyond the pale,
and every once in a blue
feckless moon, the breeze
would skitter a skirt and expose
the silhouette of a slit intersecting
a thigh – and so the afternoons
passed, and Summers died.

Somewhat

For my Great-Aunt Let in loving memory

My Great-Aunt Let
was somewhat deaf
when she wished to be, and resorted
to a state-of-the-art hearing
device to announce it, but at family
gatherings she'd seek out
a forlorn corner of the kitchen,
turn the devilish instrument off,
complain loudly of being
ignored, until her pity-lip
trembled and a tear tarnished
her cheek, after which
my Gran would settle in
beside her, give her the week's
gossip in tones un-minced
enough for the room, and the house
around it, to hear, and wait
for Letty's wince.

Old Maid

When I lay abed in the
aftermath of my fever,
my grandfather introduced
Bob and me to the sly
delights of *Old Maid*
and a year later to the guff-
and-bluff of five-card
Stud and the deuces-wild
bravado of *Baseball,*
and my mother, fearing I might
become a gunslinging gambler
like the uncle who just escaped
a kneecapping by the Mob,
fretted and prayed, but the only
game that whetted my whistle
was *Rumoli* with its black-and-red-
ribbed grid, where chips
were ten for a penny and it took
all afternoon for the
Ace-King pot to percolate.

Bliss-Tinged

November, 1960
For Anne in loving memory

We promenaded that night
on the Doon Pinnacle,
the autumnal wind at play
in the ginger flare of your hair,
your fingers finding solace
in mine, and the harvest moon
cruised above like a gilded
galleon in a sluggish sea,
and the stars glittered as if
the firmament itself were afire,
and their intimate glint presaged
love and its bliss-tinged
tug.

Wild Surmise

After reading a new poem by John B. Lee

A poem may be a throttled
thought some random rhyme
may soothe into sense, or a feeling
too condensed for the web
of words, but there's a honey-
peace in inked release
and in odes we compose that sing
of Keats's peak above
the dappled gap of Darien,
where we go when we need to know
what we think, or otherwise
surmise.

Unleavened

My Gran wasn't necessarily
a Christian, but she hedged her bets
by tithing Anglican and letting
the Reverend Stone settle
his vestments in her Best Room
and extol the virtues of loving
the Lord and His Only-Begotten,
and wax passionate on the gloom
of Armageddon and the heft
of unleavened bread, and when
the tea grew cold and the last
biscuit bitten, my Gran
put dibs on her getting to Heaven.

Shy Surprise

Chatham, Ontario: 1955
For Sandy, once again

I was too shy
to say "Hello," so you
did it for me, and when
I grew bold enough
to take your hand in mine,
you kindly gave it a wry
squeeze, and so, we kept on
strolling the sun-strummed
boulevards of our town
until the Summer ceased,
and with it, the season of shy
surprise and honey-love.

Catching

Butch and I watch
with jaw-dropping awe
as his uncle weaves and wobbles
on the front walk, heading
home, drunk enough
to survive supper, and sawing
the air as if he were swatting
flies about to hatch,
and finding nothing much
to latch onto, and Butch
says with a rueful grin,
"I hope whatever he's got
ain't catching."

Guffaw

For my maternal grandfather
John Leonard McWatters: 1872-1938*

This blurred, watery
photo is all I have
of my mother's father, murdered
in his sixty-sixth summer,
when I was still too young
to make mementos, but was told
he used to dandle me
on his knee and tickle my ribs
till my giggles un-jigged,
and he is smiling here
at the camera's prying eye,
his right hand caressing
a cannon some nimble-
minded soul had lugged
all the way from Lundy's
Lane and plunked it in a Sarnia
park to dazzle the denizens,
its black snub-snout
still facing down Fenians
and Yankee freebooters,
and there's an Irish twinkle
in his Irish eyes, and if
I listen with awe enough,
I think I can hear his Gaelic
guffaw

*My grandfather was murdered on June 18th
1938 in a Sarnia Speak-Easy. No-one was ever
charged for the crime.

Side by Side

For Tom in loving memory

How many evenings early,
when the moon had yet to glow,
did we lie side by side
like a pair of love-cozied
cubs in that little upper
room I named after you:
me singing like a superannuated
soprano: "O the great
ships sail," and I listen as your breathing
slows in its lonely motion,
as if it were soothed somnolent
by the seasoning of song, and by the time
I crescendo to the "Ally, Ally oooh,"
you have drifted into the green valley
of your dreams.

Raucous

In the lull between our Saturday
sagebrush sagas, a tuxedo-
cloaked bloke under a
black topper with his girl
Friday in tow, took
the stage like Mandrake
the Magician and the nubile Narda
and dazzled all with a flick
of his bloom-producing baton,
and silver dollars exiting
his ears and disappearing
in the gist of his fist, but when
his gal-pal shook
his topper, peered inside
and declared it empty, we held
our collective breath for the drum-
rolling abracadabra
as this doyen of legerdemain
pulled a rabbit out of his hat,
pink-eyed, blinking
and very much surprised
at our child-wild, raucous
applause.

Somewhat

For my Great-Aunt Let in loving memory

My Great-Aunt Let
was somewhat deaf
when she wished to be, and resorted
at last to a state-of-the-art
hearing device, but at family
gatherings she'd seek out
a forlorn corner of the kitchen,
turn the devilish instrument off,
complain loudly that she was being
ignored until her pity-lip
trembled and a tear tarnished
her cheek, after which
my Gran would park beside her
and give her the gossip in tones
un-minced enough for the room
and the house around it, to hear –
and wince.

Telltale

Our favourite game on grand-
father's spacious acre
was squat-tag, because
the girls, in their rush to be
un-IT, let their skirts
ride up as far as their whats-its,
then sag with a sigh, primly
pleasing, above the mottled
knobs of their knees, and though
we ought to have looked
away from such corrupting
sights, we eyed them
with a stiff-limbed vim,
waiting for the telltale
blush – to erupt.

Vintage

September 1939

In this vintage family
photo, framed by a leafing
tree and pastured grass,
my father stands in tunic
and brass, the crease in his trousers
stiff enough to cut,
and my Gran beside him,
where's she's been for his twenty-three
summers, the hair she lost
when her daughters died at birth,
now thinned by the wind,
and my Grandpa next, shoulders
back, chest out,
chin up, as if he were still
on parade, and behind them,
a matched pair of uncles,
attempting to look avuncular:
my Potsy, yet to assume
his tall-man's posture
and my Tom, who would soon endure
the obscene-ed greenery of Belgium
and the welter of war, and my heart
still stutters when I see them
as they were, caught in the camera's
unerring eye, their genes
asleep in mine.

Beguiling

For Sandy and that summer

You were looking for a guy
to while the summer away,
and I for a girl who would widen
my smile, and I don't know who
found who (and shucked their shy),
but there we were, holding
hands like a pair of apprentice
lovers, strolling the golden
boulevards of gay Paree
in Harlequinessing garb,
loving the gentle in the other's
eye, and should Autumn undo
summer's bright beguiling,
seasons to come will burnish it
anew.

Moniker

For Pussy Carr in fond memory

Ruby Carr, who preferred
cuddly kittens to kids,
nicknamed her only-
begotten "Pussy," and the ill-
dubbed son soon
found himself, dukes-up
in the schoolyard, ringed
round with taunting choristers,
chanting "Pussy is a woosie!"
and if Ruby happened to be
cruising by on her barnacled
bike, looking for rags
or other flotsam to feather
her flagging one-chick
nest, Pussy would wave
like an exuberant poodle, as if
the moniker she'd saddled him with
was good enough to be bottled.

Hooked

In Sunday school we learned
that Jesus anointed Peter,
(soon-to-be a saint)
a fisher of men, and I pictured
that awesome apostle, with rod
and reel in hand, tossing
his baited barb into Galilee's
fulsome fathom, angling
not for herring or cod,
but the souls of the lost and the glory
of God, hoisting them up,
one by one, hooked
by the chin, and grinning.

Rant

My father ranted daily
over "money-grubbing Jews"
and their roundabout snouts,
but exempted his tailor from such
an opprobrious drubbing because
he sold my Dad a ten-dollar
suit for eight with a generous
layaway plan, but on other
days his particular pique
was aimed at comedian Thomas
and his Hebrew beak, and was not
particularly pleased when I pointed out
that Danny was born Lebanese,
as Christian as Christ's disciples.

Cat-Happy

When we fostered a pair
of tiger-striped kittens
(all marmalade and whiskers),
they were as different as chalk is
from cheddar: while Peggy was a
homebody who preferred to curl up
on the likeliest lap to be stroked
and dozed, Peachy, each morning,
would cross the road to get
to the park beyond, where she out-
manoeuvred mice, meandering
moles and the odd robin,
and one day, when she zigged
when she ought-to-have zagged on route
to her derring-do, her sister,
out, at last, from under
her sibling's humbling thumb,
shucked her shyness, grew bold
and bossy, and lived for another
dozen cat-happy years.

Tipperary

When the Sunday supper had settled,
we gathered in Gran's front
room (shuttered except
for the odd afternoon
when the Reverend Stone intoned
about tithing and God)
and there, uncles and aunts
and all, we sang the old
and truest tunes in home-
spun harmony: like the soaring
chords of "Danny Boy,"
the doleful diminuendo
of that "Long, Long Trail,"
or the loping lilt of "Tipperary"
and when the singalong threatened
to lag, my Grandpa would rise,
clear his throat and serenade us
solo, his Adam's apple
bobbing like a lithe bobbin,
and I realized then that music
was something that simmered in the soul.

Battle-Scarred

Sarnia Township: 1948

When we moved to the country,
we fostered a coal-black
cat, whom we, unaware
of the racial slur, named
Nig, and he was a night owl,
prowling the friendly fields
nearby for miscellaneous
mice or meandering moles,
and should he, by chance or design,
come whisker-to-whisker
with the neighbour's terrible tom,
the fur would fly (mostly
Nig's) and the racket they raised
was a chorus of yodelling yowls
and jigging indignities – loud
enough to marinate the moon,
and when the dawn finally
broke, our ebony pet
came back – battle-scarred,
and purring.

To the Hilt

When January thawed, Leckie's
saturated fallow froze
right over, a glittering,
glazed membrane, broken
only by the black bulge of a
far horizon, where we skated
likes synchronized sylphs
thru the star-harbouring dark,
leaving, behind us, filigrees
of frond and the scarred targets
our blades made, and somewhere
ahead, where winds wilted,
the world might vanish, but we
were addicted to speed and buoyancy
of bone, and welcomed whatever
the yawning beyond might bring
to those who hallowed to the hilt.

Wince

In the Edward Street school,
silence was the order of our mornings
because Missus Duncan liked
to hear a pin drop
(if it wasn't too violent a plink),
and she had ears like an elephant's
uncle that caught the slightest
lisp of a whisper, or a nibbed
pen, dribbling ink
on a protesting page,
or a cough about to be offered,
but one day, our quilted
quietude was interrupted
by the squalid bawling of a
misbehaving boy
being strapped down the
hall, in fine Dickensian
style, and the collective gasp
of the class was loud enough
to make the Missus wince –
then smile.

Moo Cow

For Margaret Turnbull
with fond memories

Margaret "Moo Cow"
Turnbull, whose curls wouldn't
but her lip did, grew
too big for her bones
and walked with an awkward
stalking-lurch after the
little-ones teasing her
across the schoolyard, just
to see her dance like a drunk
duckling, looking for a place
to perch, and what sizzled
in her brown cow-eyes
was not anger but the kind
of mocking hoot that says,
"See me! I'm here!"

Gotcha!

Our purebred Himalayan
was affronted whenever I called her
"Cookie," raising her Himalayan
hackles in a wrathful blur
of fur and giving me a look
that said, "I'm nobody's pampered
pet," and deciding, early on,
that I wasn't exactly attracted
to cats or their kind, and took,
instead, a liking to her mistress
and the daily nosh of *Whiskers*
and petting enough keep
her purr a-churning, and on warm
summer mornings, she could be
found sunning her prized
pelt on our scalding walk,
paws upraised, belly
bowed, waiting for some
feline-friendly lass
to come along and give it
a public rub, only
to find her fingers clamped
in a four-clawed 'Gotcha!'

Fenicular*

For both of my Bobs: brother and uncle:
In loving memory

I wasn't too fenicular
about the burden of a baby
brother, but the stork flew
one in anyway: an apple-
cheeked cherub who rubbed
the sheen from my shine,
and my uncle, chary of another
Bob, christened him Googie
after some comic stooge
in the Funny Papers, and Googie
it was to all and sundry,
and like many an oddly dubbed
toddler, he grew lovingly
into his name, and I forgave
the unaborted stork.

A Wounding in the Soul

For Tom in loving memory

O Tom! Your lonely going
has left me with an ache so
wounding in my soul the gods
themselves must leave its grieving
undug, and I think of Jesus
weeping in Gethsemane's gnarled
garden, His tears sorrowing
"even unto death," a stone's
throw from His Maker and Peter's
Apostled gawp, and the blood-
love we shared for thirty
years or more was touched
by the gift of Agape,
no bereavement could unabide
or stop me from wanting to hug you
whole again.

Burst

Each winter-kneaded
seed, whatever greenery
seethes inside, must first
be ruptured by April's scathing
rain, and release its fledgling
filigree to leaf and plume
in uncorrupted burst,
and so, too, a poem
must bleed before it blooms.

Ack-Ack

Point Edward: April 1945

We thought some Jerry
in a Junker must've wandered
off-course and dropped
his lethal load on the souls
beneath, so ear-splitting
was the blast that shivered windows
and curry-combed the grass,
and like Leacock's pachyderm,
we dashed off in all directions,
peering skyward for the bomber's
doleful drone or an ack-acking
tracer, and when the air-raid
siren shredded the silence,
we were certain our Doomsday
had dawned, and what relief
to find it was only the Reverend
Bell striking a match
in a roomful of gas, seeking
no doubt a shortcut to Heaven
but landing instead, unsinged
and beaming, on his Presbyterian
ass

Coddled

For Tom in loving memory

O Tom! You were the love-
child we dreamed of, a gift
from the parsimonious gods,
whom we coddled from crib
to bib, and you gave us back
your toddler's smile with its wild
beguiling, and you were ever
estranged from the world that welcomed you,
as if you'd sensed the secret
of its disembodied, illicit
tick, and we wanted so much
for you to brandish our name
in a fresh century, plant
your progeny deep in its lush
loam, and compose them
melodious odes until
your age claimed you – asleep
at last, in the harbouring arms
of angels.

Bobbin

It must've been my brother
Bob who coaxed the girls
next door into "Show me
yours and I'll reply
with mine!" because I was as shy
as a kitten smitten with a fly,
and when the boldest lassie
eased her undies down
like a stripper testing her tease,
what should have stunned us blind
between her thighs was just
a pinkish pout, like the petals
of a closed rose, too snug
to come undone, and when,
like a gentleman, I dropped my drawers
and offered my bobbin to the air
and all, someone behind me
snickered and said, "I didn't
think they came that small."

Final Fling

For my father in loving memory

As a final fling at father-
and-son bonding, my Dad
chooses to show me the knack
of handling a thirty-ought-six,
a gun more often used
to stun a bison or stop
a burly pachyderm
in its tracks than counter-jabbing
rabbits, and when we reach
the family woodlot: master
and apprentice, aficionado
and untested tyro, a target
is tacked to a tree trunk
twenty paces away,
and with the rifle in my ginger grip,
I 'sight' the 'bull's eye'
like Davy Crockett frolicking
on the wild frontier, and jig
the trigger, and when my shoulder
un-shudders itself and resumes
its duties, my father gives me
a wry smile and says,
  "You missed the tree," then adds,
with a kind of fond regret,
"By a mile."

Solo

I saw her there but once
and that was more than enough:
Marybelle Cooper
curled on the sun-strummed
sands of Canatara
in her one-piece suit,
clinging to her girlish curves
like a lover's ruffling hands,
and I spent the rest of my day
humming without pause
like Orpheus on his lute, and singing
solo to Cupid's apt
applause.

Whee!

With a nod to E.E.

We watch the dark-eyed
carny blowing up
balloons, his thick-lidded
gawk, squeezed tight
against the illume of light,
the hiss of his breath, alive
in those plosive globes
of greens and golds and blues
a-glister, but when his gnarled
and coveting knuckles begin
to knead these perfect
worlds into writhing, bodiless
bloom, something within us
shudders voluptuous,
its mimicking, mischievous melody
fluttering
far
and
Whee!

Toe to Toe

For Tom in loving memory

You were such a cheerful
toddler, bouncing toe
to toe across the living-
room rug, loving
its elastic grasp, pleased
at last, to be upright,
joyfully buoyant and self-
propelled, and the grin you proffer
with cherub-cheeked aplomb
leaves me chuffed enough
to call the good gods
down and give them a hug.

Gentleman

*For James**

You were the first brown-
eyed babe to shinny up
the family tree, the glance
that brimmed above your cherubed
cheeks, as bright as a love-
rubbed, Christmas nut,
and there was always something
of the imp in you, as if
the world you welcomed in
was too prim to leave
untouched by the dimpled
whimsy you brought to ravel it,
and you were ever a body
in motion, as if muscles
were made to flex and tussle,
and bones to keep them afloat,
but most of all, you grew up
like a true-limbed tamarack,
and put the "gentle" back
in gentleman.

*My grandson, James Spence

Halloo

Shirley. the perennial girl-
next-door, learned to flirt
before she knew what pent
passions her batting lashes
unleashed, blaming the breeze
for teasing her skirts illicitly
aloft, and the boys for ogling
the sliver of satin that kept
her thighs from lewdly colluding,
and when she ventured the smile
she took to be her come—
hither look, promising
mischievous bliss, something
inside us shivered with shame,
shook itself loose, and hallooed
the moon.

Beguiling

For Sandy and that summer

You were looking for a guy
to while the summer away,
and I for a girl who would widen
my smile, and I don't know who
found who (and shucked their shy),
but there we were, holding
hands like a pair of apprentice
lovers, strolling the golden
boulevards of gay Paree
in Harlequinessing garb,
loving the gentle in the other's
eye, and should Autumn undo
summer's bright beguiling,
seasons to come will burnish it
anew.

Aunt Fanny

The most dyspeptic epithet
of opprobrium, during the days
when words were the weapon of choice
among boistering boys –
was "Smart aleck," or "Don't
be one," lobbed by somebody
bigger or more parental,
the ultimate putdown when the
canniest comeback was
"So's yer Aunt Fanny!"

Oga-Ooga

For Tom in loving memory

O how we loved our Raffi
and the bubbling thrum of
"Baby beluga in the deep
blue sea" with its trilling
syllables and triphammer patter,
and we sang along in frenzied
fugue till we were daffy
with laughter and a-jig with giggles,
and there is something in such
mirthful music and zany
cadence that beckons in the blood
and brings us back to be born
anew, where we are so
dazzled in the other's delight
we can't tell a decibel from an
ooga-ooga horn.

Cindered

The Boys' cindered side
of the Edward Street school
(not a blade of grass nor a shiver
of shade to idle the eye)
was littered with Big Kids
nobody diddled with,
wannabe bullies, picking out
victims, ordinary Joes
who just couldn't be bothered,
and junior losers like me,
looking for some place
to hide, like the neighbourly nook
with the prickled brick wall
we played 'potsies' from
for a penny, and, loth
to leave our niche, hunkered
down, and hoped for growth.

Haloed

When I first saw Jesus
in motion, He was afloat
on a green felt-board
and Missus Anderson's hand
nearby, plucking from her lap
the saints, Peter and Paul,
and placing them pertly beside Him,
as if they all were heading
to the Last Supper and were
fashionably late, and I wondered
why the Lord had no
halo to make His soul
shine, as He did on our Sunday-
school windows, among His
lambs, pastured in glass,
but when she read the Bible's
stirring account of that green
bucolic scene, the figures
came alive in my malleable mind,
and I thought they were the stuff
of something magical –
haloed or not.

Harbour

For Anne in loving memory

If I should die before
I wake, forsaking daylight
for the dark, something akin
to my soul will navigate
those dim corridors,
and swim like a new-finned
'puffer' in a sea, ruffled
by love, and find my heart's
harbour in thee.

Galilean

In Sunday school, we learned
about the Galilean Sea
where St. Peter and his pals
fished for their daily bread
and Jonah was welcomed by a whale
and Jesuss trolled for souls
in barefoot bravado,
and none of us thought to ask
if the cachelot coughed up his dinner
or Peter hooked enough fare
to cater a Supper or Christ
found knaves and nimrods
enough to save from sin
or impress transgressors like me.

And I was One

Every second, somewhere
on Earth's fecund-ian girth,
lovers succumb, and the world
is reawakened in the fevered
weave of a womb, where a
passion-pummeled seedling,
no bigger than a pygmy-possum's
thumb, gives birth to itself,
and thus are millions spun
out of such love-lit beginnings,
and I was one.

Brim

For Anne in loving memory

If I were to sketch you yet
again, I'd let my pencil,
like Leonardo's lustrous brush,
limn your loveliness
in lines of lush allure,
but even so, it would take
a fledgling Caravaggio
or besotted Botticelli
or hectic Van Eck to capture
the gamine's glance you gave me,
like a gift, each morning,
to reawaken my world
and bring it, bubbling, to the brim.

If You had Lived

For Tom in loving memory

I you had lived but a few
years longer, it would've been me
who died and you who suffered
the oozing wound of losing
someone too dear to let go –
your bereavement pain, sea-
seething inside you: bone-
bruised, blood-ruddered,
bliss-blind, and now,
mine.

Sketching Anne, Again

If I were sketching you again,
I'd call upon the charmed art
of Varley or a born-again
Gainsborough or Raphael's
graphic knack, and your Mona
Lisian smile would bloom
thru the Ages like a daffodil
stunned young by the sun,
and break a hundred hearts
before it fractured mine.

Pooch

My dog Moochie was a pooch
without a pedigree, bat lack
of a lordly lineage couldn't
keep the uppity from his mutt's
strut, and though his webbed
toes suggested "water
spaniel" somewhere
in pater's genes, he kept
a fraught distance between him
and the weed-congested ditch
that dogged our roadside,
and should some arrogant auto
or cycling savant deign
to stray upon that sacred
terrain, my pup, like a proper
cop, would make a teeth-
gnashing dash for the nearest
offending tire and bite it
till it ceased or surrendered,
and I loved him even more
after my father dropped him
off, distempered and bewildered,
on some empty township
lot, where, bereft of doggy
breath, he could die a dog's
death.

Moxie

The Reverend Bell was famous
everywhere in the Point
for the flurry in his Sunday sermons
and the length of his doleful
Doxologies, long before
the fateful day he detected
gas, lit a match, and blew
his manse to the Kingdom Come
he promised in every prayer
to those Presbyterian enough
to warrant the Lord's blessing
and a personal pew among the
select Elect, and when
he waltzed away from the doomed
ruin, we pictured ourselves
wannabe parsons with a bit
of God's pluck and all
of His moxie.

Opulent

Sarnia Township: 1948

It must've been four o'clock
that Christmas morn
because the lights in Leckie's
barn across the way were glowing
lonesome in the immense density
of the dark, and cows inside
with their opulent udders were lowing,
and the moon had long ago
conceded the sky to the high
hegemony of the stars – while I
lay wide awake, desperate
to be dreaming, but listening,
still, for the plump chatter
of hooves above, or a reindeer's
neigh, or an elvesian chuckle,
or a cheerleading ho-ho,
while a million miles from anywhere,
a babe in a Bethlehem stable
was born to save us from Santa's
gilded grasp – and ourselves.

Nimbling

The cumulonimbi that loomed
above the Lake all after-
noon at last release
what has been seething inside them,
and snow comes thrashing
down upon the town
in wind-dizzied filigree
that soon consumes the green
grit of the grass, and curls
itself up on sills and eaves
into a kind of blanched,
dreamless sleep, and just
before the final flake
falls, children erupt
nimbling in their ease, as if
something in snow or the silence
it engenders, speaks the language
of the body-unbound
and the child's wild awaking.

Gothic

Chatham, Ontario:
December 24, 1953

Darkness had already fallen
with no wind to flutter it,
not even a wee wheeze
where it was welcome, and it
began to snow: furred
flakes in filigreed mis-
array, afloat on their own
winsome weight, and just
ahead, St. Patrick's cathedral —
steeple, belfry, buttress
all — was a ghostly, Gothic
blur, as if some over-
zealous Van Gogh had dreamed it
into being, and in that dis-
embodied moment, I could almost
believe there was a God.

Hallowed Eve

Christmas 2022

There is always something
hallowed about Christmas Eve,
when the stars glitter as they did
above Bethlehem and the mangered
Babe amid the shallowed
breathing of beasts and inkling
of Kings, and for a holy moment
our sin-bitten world
is un-estranged and,
hearkening to the news, undoes
the dark in our heathen hearts.

The other Garden

Christmas day: 2022

Christmas morning breaks
as if no other day
would do, with snow enough
to have soothed Santa's patient
sleighing, and children come
tumbling from the cozy abode
of their dreams to celebrate
a Saviour's virgin birth
and thank Saint Nick for the
beribboned gifts beneath
the trimmed, bebaubled tree,
but elsewhere on a troubled Earth
some squalid toddler
paws at the rubbled ruin
of his home in search of bread
or affexction, peace or sleep,
and once again, in the garden
of His Gethsemane, Jesus
weeps.

Something Other

For Marilyn Matheson-Steele

All of your friends prayed
for a birthday pony, but you
took the prize itself:
a shaggy Shetland, as black
as bitumen fresh from the
coal-face, and christened it
"Champ," and rode it like one
in your Dale Evans duds
with the silver spurs that glittered
like crystal in a klieg-lamp's
lasering light, and when
you galloped by, thighs
astride and pertly pummelled,
my heart skittered off-course,
and hammered for something other
than the horse.

One Club Short

For Gerry Parker: In Memoriam

When you and I combed
*Sunningdale's** groomed greenery
in search of the perfect pin-
high pitch or the lip-
hugging putt, I watched
in awe as your drives bevelled
in the breeze like a bird in feathered
flight, and the way your wedges
struck the turf with a crisp
command that sent the dimpled
missile aloft, wherever
you willed it to go, and O
the grin you gave a duffer
like me when it dropped
with a plop an inch from the flag,
but more often than not,
bursting with a bravura I much
admired (and a flawless torque
and tempo), you'd choose a Nine
when an Eight would nicely do
and, with the practiced aplomb
of a pro, leave the shot
one club short.

*A golf course north of London, Ontario

No Better Joy

For Gerry Parker in loving memory

You were such a loving leprechaun
of a man with a dance in every
step you took to bring
delight to those privileged
enough to know you,
and the gods granted you
a cornucopia of talents:
a flair for the fathomless felicities
of drama and the actor's tactful
craft (home-truths
you passed along to a generation
of students, 'rapt withal'),
with an ear for the luminous moods
of music so finely tuned
you tickled the ivories but once
and they bounced to your bravado,
and so, you turned your artist's
eye to pen and 'parchment,'
and dotted your thoughts in inklings
of ink, like a passionate Pissarro,
but what I remember most
(besides the sweet ease
of your seven-iron) is the day
you took our fatherless Tom
in your arms and jiggled his giggle,
as if there were no better
joy this side of Heaven.

Great and Otherwise

When I have met my Maker,
if He or She will have me,
the names of my innumerable
aunts and uncles, great
and otherwise, who peopled
picnics in the park, reunions
in rumpus rooms, Christmas
concerts in the township hall
and clan gatherings once
in a blue-eyed moon,
came alive for me
in stories told so often
they might have been true –
and all – their filial fame
notwithstanding - will follow me
to the grave, but someone,
somewhere, the puzzled cousin
of some superannuated aunt,
perhaps, will pause, say "Ah!"
and remember them into being
again.

Apple Pie

For my grandmother:
Ethel Cookson Reeve Gutteridge
1888-1957

It never once occurred
to my ten-year-old
unenquiring mind
that my Gran was anything other
than the denizen downstairs
who hugged me when my heart hurt,
plied me with cod-liver malt
to keep my sniffles iffy
and my stamina stalwart,
mixed us jugs of *Freshie*
we peddled for pennies to our parched
chums when the Summer clung,
and baked us apple pies
on Sunday mornings in lieu of
Church and its pious pews,
and none of us knew that she'd
been a homeless waif, dumped
by a drunken mother onto the
teeming streets of London,
and rescued there by a good-
neighbouring clan, who piggy-
backed her to America, passing
her off as a sibling Reeve,
a surname she took and proudly
kept like a tender talisman,
and thus, bequeathed me
more than a dozen assorted
ersatz uncles, aunts
and cousins to pin on the family
tree, and never once
wonder why, like my Gran
with her apple-dappled pie.

Hooked

In Sunday school we learned
that Jesus appointed Peter,
soon-to-be made saint,
a fisher of men, and I pictured
that awesome apostle, with rod
and reel, flicking his baited
barb into Galilee's fulsome
fathom, angling not
for herring or cod, but souls
of the lost and the glory of God,
bringing them up, one
by one, hooked by the chin,
and grinning.

Madcap

For Tom in loving memory

O how you loved our after-
supper muppetry - its mad-
cap tomfoolery
and shameless shenanigans,
and you were ever amused
when the critics from their lofty boxes
interrupted Fozzie and his stuttering
sputter, and you chortled at Miss
Piggy in her uppity rig
and porcine whine, and at the
Swedish cook, uncorking
his "Bork! Bork!" – and Gonzo's
throttled contortions brought
a grin to your eyes I could've
bottled, but it was the
frantic antics of the pettifogging
Frog that widened our smile
the most- and these risible
love-tugging moments
still dance inside,
long after the laughter
stopped, and you died.

Frantic Antics

For Tom in loving memory

As I'd done with both of my own,
when evenings softened with the sun,
I opened my well-thumbed
Winnie-the-Pooh, and began
to read, listening for your giggle
when Piglet found Pooh,
fresh from a treacle-licking
schtick, stumping about
with the honey-pot still
on his noggin like a stoppered
bottle, and the wee beastie
wheezed his breathless "It's a
heff – heff -heffalump!"
and raced right home
and put himself to bed,
and you guessed all along
that hives at the top of trees
were certain to have bees unfriendly
to bears and happy to sting
gadabout snouts, and O
how you chuckled when Eeyore
brayed his glum harumph
when the nail that attached his tail
failed, and Tigger's bounce
was bigger than his bound,
and I caught you scowling
when Owl delivered his Sunday
sermon or waxed pedantic,
and if you could've, you'd have
followed Christopher Robin
home and settled down
in the Hundred Acre Wood.

Bliss Enough

For Sandy and that summer

That summer of our fancied
romance, every step
we dared, palm in pilgrim
palm, seemed to be bathed
in Heaven's condoling glow,
and I was pleased to play
Galahad to your queenly Guin,
and like ruffed-up royalty,
we strolled out streets holy,
and the winsome kiss you shared,
and the glance that gilded it,
were bliss enough.

Bouquets

It must've been in the summer
of 'forty-four, the War
still seething its heathen
horrors, when Mister Robinson,
next door, brought
his box-Brownie over
and snapped this photo
of Gran and my improbably
young mother, their arms
a-burst with bloom and buoyant
bouquet that one son
or another, from some faraway
faded barracks, blew
a week's wages upon
just to prompt these
widening smiles, and lance
his loneliness.

Upstart

I spoke too soon,
before the thought I thought
I had was ripe for revelation
in the prism'd presence of a poem,
but I was pleased that I had
done so because the flawed
awe of my upstart words
had found a home wherethey
were wanted: in the surprised smile
of one who'd waited too long
to catch my meaning

We All Go Alone

For Tom in loving memory

O Tom! Wherever your soul
has flown, weep not
for me in my bereavement
pain, for each pang
that pierces some fresh portion
of my heart brings you singing
back to me, keeps
your smile alive in mine,
and though we all go alone
into the hearkening dark,
we are warmed on the way
by thoughts of those we loved
who got there ahead of us.

Artful

For Becca

Like some artful Greco-
Roman wrestler, squeezed
into a taut, trim body,
you take your combatant's stance
in the middle of the mat, staring
down all comers,
and before we can say "Gotcha!"
you've got the burly girl
opposite in a high-crotch
hold, then take a Saturday-
night-ride to the winning
pin – capturing the gold,
and our hearts.

A Birthday Poem

For Kevin*: February 20, 2023

You were the runt of the litter,
a bouncing blue-eyed
boy when a red-headed
daughter was wanted, but the smile
you bedizened rooms with,
announced to a doubting world
that you had arrived in style,
undaunted, and no number
of brood-brothers would ever
blunt the glitter of the grin
you gave us, *gratis*, every
day since, and made joy
your calling-card.

*Kevin is my youngest grandson

Cheers

On Grandfather's lawn,
Shirley, the slim-limbed,
chimp-chested girl-
next-door, mimics
the strip-tease she sees
in the sassy mirror of her mind,
and gives us what passes for
a bawdy, hip-swivelling
bump-and-grind, and the boys,
in lieu of a leer, politely
applaud, even though
we can't be sure such
thrashing, adult actions
deserve a giggle or a cheer.

Ink-Brushed

For Anna Yin

You offer to translate a dozen
of my poems into ancient Chinese,
and I imagine my verse as ink-
brushed slashes in their picto-
graphic simplicity, like just-
bred syllables scrawled
on a Neanderthalian wall
to be read in some far
century, when words have lost
their lustre, by a mendicant
mandarin with a passion for poetry
and the prick of its puzzle

When the Gloaming Lets Go

There was always something
unsettled when the gloaming
let go and the dark came down
on Monk and Michigan like a
shudder, and Mara's lamp
blinked on like a marigold moon,
and under its lean light
it was ever hide-and-go-seek
with the summer humming inside
and our bones afloat, while all
the while, the night-sky
was harvesting stars, and somewhere,
further than far, the vast
firmament winked at our wondering,
and the gods who bred us, beguiled.

February 14, 2023

For Anne in loving memory

You never cared much
for beribboned candy or boxed
chocolate or the saccharine sentiments
of greeting-card kitsch
or Hallmark's jogging doggerel,
but on the off-chance
I might put the "Oh!"
back in "romance," I bring you
a dozen red roses,
fresh from the garden my heart,
where you, O mistress mine,
have always been my Valentine.

Long Before

Long before there were
affordable vacuums to suck
the dust from dirt-drugged
rugs, our Sunday carpets
were hung in the sunshine,
whereupon my gran began
whacking them with a webbed-
wire weapon some unreformed
Nazi might condone,
till the knap collapsed and a winter's
worth of tread surrendered
in little gasps that clung
to the bend in the breeze, then
swooned in the hapless grass,
and Gran would give me
her best grandma-grin,
as if to say, "You just haveta
have the knack."

Whittling

Wordsworth thought the world
was too much with us,
but when we were young and hungry
for whatever the world wrought us,
we lived by our wits from day
to day, untouched by anything
odd in the bone, and giving birth
to ourselves like novice gods
cloning the cosmos, certain
that all our sonnets rhymed
and our flags furled, as we whittled
our time away.

A Nickel's Worth

For Effie Free in memoriam

Every summer morning
whether the sun simmered
or not, Effie Free,
five years old and counting,
left home for a hop, skip
and jump across the road
with a nickel in her fist for a
singe-dip or a bagful
of teasing sweets, till the day
a cruising Cadillac caught her
on a bound, and she lay there
on the cold pavement like a dropped
doll somebody forgot,
her little lean life
lopped.

Bee-Stung

The girls of the Point, when we
were young and yearning, were long-
legged, lanky waifs
in whirled skirts that barely
disguised the nobbiness of their knees,
but somehow, we knew
that curves would emerge in prurient
places, and batted lashes
prompt improbable urges,
and lust, like a bee-stung
goblin, hobnob with our hearts.

Surprise
With a nod to Emily D

A poem is a thought that ought
to be a surprise to everyone
but the poet who put it
superbly there, thinking
no doubt that the words
he wielded would convey the gist
of what he wished to say,
etched, as they were, in ink,
but somehow, they came
, in the rhyme
or dithered ado in the rhythms,
and whether they now be ballad
or extolling ode, they are deemed
to mean, and truth – their prize.

Prothalamium*

For Shahrzad and Tim
(with a nod to Shakespeare's Sonnet 116)

Yours will be the marriage
of true minds, as the Bard
once rhapsodized:
two souls seeing
a world in the other's eyes,
and no impediment to your live-
long love shall be admitted,
for yours is the star the Heavens
were made to solemnize,
and may your happiness and the hope
it portends never to Time's
bending sickle succumb,
or let it impair the joys
that quicken the conjugal bed.

*A song to celebrate an upcoming wedding

Backward

With a nod to Keats and John B. Lee

When I am seized by the full
fury of a poem giving birth
to itself, the words come not
like a flood that drowns them
till they utter, but rather as a
sun-stroked rose
bled backward to the bud.

Some Names

Some names survive the thwarting
thickets of the past with all
the memories, sweet or not,
still attached – like *Susan Coote*
for one: astride her birthday
bike on the private preserve
of my walk, and there I am:
feet splayed, arms
akimbo, full of my seven-
year self, blocking
her way, and I feel some
soaring satisfaction
at the fear I prompt in her surprise,
and when she meekly retreats,
I am shaken with a shame
that suddenly has a name:
bully.

Drummer

For Shirley McCord

Shirley sets the stage
for her drum majorette's
vignette with a high-stepping
strut that shows the gathered
gawkers a shimmer of thigh
and lots of girly crotch,
while all the while twirling
her baton like a fervid Dervish,
and when she's done her princely
prance, we don't know whether
to whistle or hum.

A Good Hug

Varsity Stadium, Toronto:
November, 1957

My roommate sets me up
with his city cousin on a blind
date for the "big game,"
and we sit side by side
on the wind-blown bleachers,
huddled close, more
for the warmth than anything
hotly erotic, and I am
pleased to feel her mittened
hand in mine, and out
on the frozen field, the brutal
ballet of rugby football
unfolds, and when the gridiron
Goliaths hear our chuffed
cheering, it's as if the hail
of our hoorays was more than enough
to unleash the beast in the blood,
when all they really needed
was a good hug.

Womb-Words

When first I began to rhyme
the potted thoughts that would not
let me be, I believed
that poems came down
in a mind-numbing flood,
as if some lexical dam
had burst and loosed the whirlwind
of its womb-words, but now
I know they come with a niggle,
an itch, a tentative tug,
nudging their way towards the teem
of meaning – which only the poet
can plumb in sonnet, ballad
or slow-honed ode,
his budget of tropes bigger
than a beau's hopes.

Nine for Anne

In loving memory

Come and Lie Beside Me

Come and lie beside me
and let the morning alight
like a bride's blush, and I
shall hold your hand in mine
like a talisman of all we've been
and done since first we bid
our bodies be, and plumbed
their blithe bedight, and in
the hush of this day's
praise, love is again
begun and olden souls
reborn.

Bliss-Tinged

November, 1960

We promenaded that night
on the Doon Pinnacle,
the autumnal wind at play
in the ginger flare of your hair,
your fingers finding solace
in mine, and the harvest moon
cruised above like a gilded
galleon in a sluggish sea,
and the stars glittered as if
the firmament itself were afire,
and their intimate glint presaged
love and its bliss-tinged
tug.

Ever Enough

Be still, my love, upon
your silken pillow, and let
the moonlight gild us
in its ghostly glow, for this
is the hour we are most alive:
our thawed bodies but a breath's
effort apart, beyond the
dark's erotic reach,
and we can feel the kneading
beat of the other's heart,
and all thought of the day
now done, with its fits and starts,
is ebbed and moot, and we are
free to dream as we will,
certain that under anyone's
sun, love is ever
enough.

Yours to Keep

Lay your bending brow
upon my pillow, and I will
kiss you softly to sleep,
where, worlds away,
you may dream, perhaps, of me,
now and then, and of love
that laps itself, and lofts:
a bliss above the day's
endearment, and when
you wake, I'll still be here –
yours to keep.

Quite Sure

You weren't quite sure
what it meant to be married
to a budding, breathing poet,
and so, I eschewed reading
aloud my latest darlings
or boasting of the blandishments
in my maiden review, but you,
while keeping a wary watch
on my exotic jottings, knew
there was something *other* in me
that needed to fend in its own
furrow, and I still recall
the day you said to our bright-
eyed, curly haired boy,
who'd questioned the frequency
of my Parnassian peregrinations,
"He belongs to the world," and I was
sure she was quite.

Bliss-Tinged

November, 1960

We promenaded that night
on the Doon Pinnacle,
the autumnal wind at play
in the ginger flare of your hair,
your fingers finding solace
in mine, and the harvest moon
cruised above like a gilded
galleon in a sluggish sea,
and the stars glittered as if
the firmament itself were afire,
and their intimate glint presaged
love and its bliss-tinged
tug.

Tiptoe

Once again, I gaze
on this lovingly framed
photo, the lone memento
of the day you widened my smile,
bride and groom on Gallina's
lawn, tilted tiptoe
as if to savour the amaze
in the other's eye; me:
in a borrowed blazer and shoes
that needed a shine, and you:
silken in wedding-white,
the windfall of your lustrous
locks, tucked up with milady's
fine-boned comb,
and I'll keep on perusing
this nuptial nudge until
my luck runs out
or the grainy patina fades
to black

Alzheimer's

It's nouns that go first,
their rounded vowels softening
at the centre, their cleaving consonants
collapsed at the frayed hem
of memory, and the objects out there
they once nominated nicely,
float free in the maelstrom
of the mind, and the faces that endeared
and kept our smile from whiling
no longer have a name, and the syllables
that sang to our infant ear
have nothing precise to say,
leaving the worded world
ajar, until, at the end,
we can't remember who we are.

First Flower

Point Edward: circa 1947

If it's almost Spring
in First Bush, the leaf-
moulded corridors and shrubbery
shadows are a-flutter with the tri-
petalled trillium, its floral
flustering as white as a novice
nun's wimple and as shy
as her cloistered smile – pushing
their budded snouts up
through the rain-rinsed
muck towards the sun's
light-licked elixir,
and we were warned by our betters
that plucking them would bring us
seven years of illicit
luck, but I wondered what
that pampered bloom would look like
in a window-box or well-
watered pot or a bride's
bouquet, forgetting that its pincered
root would come undone
at the slightest rupturing tug,
and, trusting that good luck
or ill was simply moot,
I picked my poison and carried on
as if I hadn't transgressed
some flawed canonical law.

The Canadian Prince of Poetry, Don Gutteridge, Under Full Sail: His 2023 Voyages. A Brief Sail into his Book, *Sailing with the Wind*

Miguel Ángel Olivé Iglesias, MSc
Associate Professor Holguin University, Cuba
Professor of English, Literature and Stylistics
Member of the Mexican Association of Language and Lit Professors
Author, Poet, Writer, Editor, Reviewer, Translator

We have not yet rested from prior poetic voyages with the Canadian Prince of Poetry, Don Gutteridge, and his prolific hand is already calling all hands on deck for another journey into the enthralling seas where words and poems are one in his productive mind. Wet Ink Books´ ink still feels wet with Gutteridge´s 2023 poetry books, *A Fine-Tuned Heart* and *A Bumper Crop 1 and 2*, but he pauses not and comes full sail with yet a new book, *Sailing with the Wind*. No wonder he has said that he "…seems to dream poems then wakes up writing them."

Those who have followed Gutteridge´s extraordinary writing career will immediately notice that this new rendering can be viewed as a natural continuation of his previous volumes. Gutteridge eases us into *Sailing with the Wind* confident that his old-time themes, his golden ones, won´t fail to find a place in the readers´ preference. And he is right.

He opens the book with "Apple-Cheeked," a highly emotional piece to his adored Tom. When we read this poem, we pick airs of a classic not only stirred by allusions made, "… your infant curls like Apollo's…", but in the cohesive elegance and the overall harmony that characterize a master at work. As we read on, Gutteridge recreates and re-sculpts his powerful memories of people, places, instances, events. Supported by the diary-like framework I have referred to in my previous analyses of his oeuvre, he hand-guides us into the all-encompassing appeals to the senses, where chiefly sight (also sound, onomatopoeia: "… with a grrr / for Papa's outsized growl" – from the poem "Patter") stream onto our act of reading.

Read "Cadenza," to choose one out of any other poem which would serve perfectly as an example, and be filled with complete descriptions based mostly on the expert use of epithets, simple or complex in construction:

> *"their scarobed, slug-*
> *slung bodies upward*
> *out of the home-loam*
> *and into the rarity of Summer's*
> *early air, wobbling*
> *into lopsided flight*
> *like big-bellied bombers –*
> *seduced by the slick elixir…"*

Alongside his seasoned handling of words and syntax, Gutteridge, too, seduces the frontiers of English grammar, verbal inflections or resourceful use of affixation to send his poems into different expressive byways and create novel effects. Examples of the latter are "unalive" (from "On the Prowl"), "unsmile" (from "Farewell"), "un-confusion" (from "Perpetual").

About "Perpetual," there is a meditative element that is evident to the keen reader. In readdressing an ordinary reality with a thoughtful perspective, Gutteridge invites us to reflect on the routines we humans are sometimes cocooned in:

"For a time, my only friend
was the goldfish, swimming / /
in the glass
globe of his bowl, round-
about in clockwise
un-confusion, as if
he thought there was somewhere
else to go or a place
he ought to be / /
but when he got to the spot
where it all began, he met
himself coming back..."

Is it the poet just reminiscing his childhood days? Is it a child, mature and pensive, now brought into the poet´s perpetuation of memories? Is it the poet approaching a far reality and comparing it, critically, with human realities? Whatever the real motif was for Gutteridge to write this piece, by the end of the poem we come to grips with the fact that what he narrates in the poem is the truth (in his book *A Bumper Crop*, Gutteridge says in his last poem, "Ruthless": "my rhythms run in ruthless / pursuit of the truth..."). Seeking the truth is one of Gutteridge´s greater quests. Let´s read the last part of "Perpetual" and see why there may be an obvious truth in this poem:

"... and I wondered what it might
be like to travel inside
a world perpetually circled,
without an end in sight
to make the miles worthwhile."

Whether we read other authors (I am thinking of Canadian poet Richard Grove´s *The Importance of Good Roots*, an insightful social poking into the human mind and behavior) or Don Gutteridge here and now with his "Perpetual" (in *A Bumper Crop* I commented on his social-criticism side as well), these last lines are a red flag flapping over the notion of how monotony closes in on us and devours our freedom, our capacity to go beyond or think beyond the box. One way or the other, when I read the poem, I related to this thought: "...I wondered what it might / be like to travel inside / a world perpetually circled…" The last two lines are also profoundly meaningful. They made me recall, right away, Robert Frost's lines "…and miles to go before I sleep…":

> *"… without an end in sight*
> *to make the miles worthwhile."*

Gutteridge warns that the miles (our lifespan) must be worthwhile. Human existence cannot be minimized to a happy-go-lucky, empty passage—it must have significance; it must have a purpose. The well-known American actor Denzel Washington said, "Everything that I have is by the grace of God… Do what you feel passionate about… Don't be afraid to be outside the box… to think outside the box… to dream big. But remember, dreams without goals are just dreams, so have dreams but have goals…" (*taken from a Commencement Speech at Dillard University - New Orleans, U.S.A.*). This is the key idea, Gutteridge realizes, and shares his concern, that life, in reference to us humans, expands beyond "the glass / globe of his bowl…" in reference to the goldfish.

I have oftentimes stated how vivid Gutteridge's memories are and how meticulous his delineations of those memories. The poem "Guffaw" stands as a special illustration of both his power of recollection and his use of language resources to create images and leave imprints. A photograph he holds of his maternal grandfather suffices to spark in him what I would call memories-by-extension, as what he writes in his poems was told to him. All in all, the poem remains solid, striking and loyal to Gutteridge's intent to perpetuate his family's stories.

In the process of remembering (by extension), the poet resorts to the senses—and feelings, which have a doubtless effect on the reader. He begins strongly:

> *"This blurred, watery*
> *photo is all I have*
> *of my mother's father, murdered*
> *in his sixty-sixth summer,*
> *when I was still too young*
> *to make mementos…"*

He emphasizes on the temporal divide between him and his grandfather by using two words, "blurred" and "watery." Then he introduces the sad occurrence, "murdered," and makes it clear that he "was still too young / to make mementos…" From then on, the happy instances he does not remember but were activated, told, by his mother:

> "… was told
> he used to dandle me
> on his knee and tickle my ribs
> till my giggles un-jigged,
> and he is smiling here
> at the camera's prying eye…"

Finally, Gutteridge visits, and takes us with him, the realm of senses, one he has frequently used in his poems (here we have sight and hearing). While doing so, he pays tribute to his origins:

> "…there's an Irish twinkle
> in his Irish eyes, and if
> I listen with awe enough,
> I think I can hear his Gaelic
> guffaw…

As we continue reading, we reencounter poems included in previous books. I am certain they have a distinct status, so much so that he decided to have them in *Sailing with the Wind*. Some of these are "Shy Surprise," "When the Gloaming Lets Go," "February 14, 2023," "Long Before," "Bliss-Tinged," etc. For my comments on these and other poems, readers may refer to *A Bumper Crop*.

Gutteridge closes this new book with a section he subtitles **Nine for Anne**. He revisits poems from his other books, from which I am re-lured to comment about "Come and Lie Beside Me."

I have made cross-references in this essay to mention other authors´ poems. With Gutteridge´s "Come and Lie Beside Me," I have fondly remembered a dear Canadian friend, Merle Amodeo, and her poem "Let Morning Never Come." Let´s read a fragment, "What bliss to wake beside you, / your arms entwined in mine. / My lips still moist from yours, / my ears attuned to your heartbeat. / Like Juliet, I fear the lark's song / and softly hum to cover its tune…" (*taken from After Love, Merle Amodeo, 2014, Copyright © 2014 by Merle Amodeo. Library of Congress. Book printed in the United States of America*). There are outstanding points of coincidence in spirit, simplicity and beauty between these two poems, let alone the intimate conversational aspect so at home with Gutteridge, that I did not want to let go unnoticed.

In my analyses of "Come and Lie Beside Me" I have stated that there is a "… superb lyrical prowess, especially in the poems dedicated to Anne. These are sweet pieces that I, a hopeless romantic, just fell for… Language and syntax, spirit and devotion render these lines a doubtless Shakespearean halo. One cannot avoid being caught in the beautiful simplicity—or the simple beauty—of the proposal and its nostalgic aura."

With this and other poems, Gutteridge ends his *Sailing with the Wind*. Those who have read him and followed his intense and extensive work will feel grateful Wet Ink Books has published another volume of the Gutteridge "saga." The Canadian Prince of Poetry maintains his magic. As R. G. Moyles (The University of Alberta, in The Journal of Canadian Poetry) says, "Literary critics will have much to say about Gutteridge's uniquely Canadian vision. I am content that his poetry is accessible, unobtrusive, delights the ear, stirs the heart and even enters into the soul. It is the art that mirrors inner life." Let´s have "sea art" then with this new book by our Don Gutteridge.

In his poem, "Defy" (*from the book Home Ground, Hidden Brook Press, 2018*), Gutteridge claimed, "… poetry is both bliss and consolation, a way of speaking to the world that subsumes both shy and defy." He has widely spoken to the world for decades, and I am sure the Muses will accompany him in his voicing and orchestration of words, rhythms and rhymes to pursue joy and find relief from the heavy, unavoidable facts of life. Gutteridge has found peace and has risen to move on and sit amongst the top writers of his generation. Thank you, Prince of Canadian Poetry. Sail safely…

Author Biographical Note:

Don Gutteridge was born in Sarnia and raised in the nearby village of Point Edward. He taught High School English for seven years, later becoming a Professor in the Faculty of Education at Western University, where he is now Professor Emeritus. He has published seventy-six individual books and several anthologies of selected works, including poetry, fiction and scholarly essays in literary criticism and pedagogical theory and practice. He has published twenty-two novels, including the twelve-volume Marc Edwards mystery series and a YA fable, The Perilous Journey of Gavin the Great, and forty-three books of poetry, one of which, Coppermine, was short-listed for the 1973 Governor-General's Award. In 1970 he won the UWO President's Medal for the best periodical poem of that year, "Death at Quebec." His poetry has been translated into Spanish by Professor, Miguel Ángel Olivé Iglesias, into Bengali by professor, Dr. Shireen Huq and into Chinese, by Poet Laureate, Anna Yin. Don lives quietly and writes daily in London, Ontario.

Email: gutteridgedoanld@gmail.com
Website: dongutteridgeauthor.ca

www.ingramcontent.com/pod-product-compliance
Lightning Source LLC
Chambersburg PA
CBHW031428120626
46545CB00006B/2315